Presented to

....

From

....

Date

Mothering by Heart

Celebrating the Moments
That Last Forever

WRITTEN BY

ROBIN JONES GUNN

PHOTOGRAPHY BY

DOROTHY PYLE

MULTNOMAH GIFTS™

Multnomah®Publishers *Sisters, Oregon*

MOTHERING BY HEART

© 1996, 2002 by Robin Jones Gunn
published by Multnomah Publishers, Inc.
P.O. Box 1720, Sisters, Oregon 97759

ISBN 1-57673-914-7

Photographs by Dorothy Pyle are reproduced under the license from Leo Licensing LLC, Cookeville, TN © 2002 by Leo Licensing LLC.

Designed by Koechel Peterson & Associates, Minneapolis, Minnesota

Multnomah Publishers, Inc., has made every effort to trace the ownership of all poems and quotes. In the event of a question arising from the use of a poem or quote, we regret any error made and will be pleased to make the necessary correction in future editions of this book.

Quote by Liane Kupferberg Carter © 1994. Used by permission.

Scripture quotations are taken from *The Holy Bible*, New International Version © 1973, 1984 by International Bible Society, used by permission of Zondervan Publishing House; *The Living Bible* (TLB) © 1971, used by permission of Tyndale House Publishers, Inc. All rights reserved; *The Holy Bible*, New King James Version (NKJV) © 1984 by Thomas Nelson, Inc.

Multnomah is a trademark of Multnomah Publishers, Inc., and is registered in the U.S. Patent and Trademark Office. The colophon is a trademark of Multnomah Publishers, Inc.

Printed in China

02 03 04 05 06 07 08 — 10 9 8 7 6 5 4 3

www.multnomahgifts.com

Table of Contents

INTRODUCTION

Do you remember the moment you knew for sure that you were pregnant?

For me that moment came when my husband, Ross, and I were sitting silently in the doctor's office. Ross reached over and took my hand in his. The doctor bustled into the room, positioned himself behind his big mahogany desk, and announced, "Your suspicions were correct. You are going to have a baby."

From that very moment, I felt changed. No longer just a woman, just a daughter, or just a wife—I was a mother. Entrusted by God to do that which is not gifted to men or even to angels. Only a woman's body can carry and nurture new life. What a privilege to be part of such a miracle! I wanted to savor every moment so that I would always remember the gift, the challenge, and the delight of being a mom.

On the advice of an older friend, I started keeping a journal. As I ventured into the woods of motherhood, that journal became like a wicker basket slung over my arm. Into that basket I tossed all kinds of treasures: reflections of childhood innocence, glimpses of the eternal, and moments of private wonder. Soon that basket was filled to

overflowing, and the day came when I was brave enough to share my journal entries with a younger friend.

"You should put this together into a book on mothering," she told me.

"Oh, no," I said. "I couldn't write a book on mothering. I had no idea what I was doing when our children were born."

"Exactly," she said. "But you did it with your whole heart, and that's what gives me hope as a new mom. I don't know what I'm doing either. But your stories encourage me to trust God more deeply and to put my whole heart into this new season of life."

With that in mind, I offer these stories to you—dear, kindred, mothering heart. May you feel encouraged as you venture into the woods of motherhood. May your path be filled with light, and may you find great delight in celebrating the moments that last forever.

Waiting

Dear Baby, here beneath my heart,
I thought that you might come today;
the timing just seemed right.
But the stars are out
and the moon is high
and sheepishly I wonder why
I try to arrange the plans of God.
For now I know
you will not come
until the One who holds eternity
rustles your soft cocoon and
whispers in tones that I will not hear,
"It's time, precious gift.
Now it's time."

I will wait on the LORD…
And I will hope in Him.
Here am I and the children
whom the LORD has given me!

ISAIAH 8:17-18, NKJV

THE FIRST TIME
I SAW YOU

Pink flesh pressed against my cheek,
Tiny fingers curled up tight,
Gentle coos of such delight—
It is no secret:
You've captured my heart.

HUSH! MY DEAR, LIE STILL AND SLUMBER,

HOLY ANGELS GUARD THY BED.

HEAVENLY BLESSINGS WITHOUT NUMBER,

GENTLY FALLING ON THY HEAD.

ISAAC WATTS

$\mathcal{T}$ENDER INTUITIONS

I hold you in my arms, young prince. You sleep in sweet, heavenly peace. Yet I wonder if you'd be so calm if you knew the truth: I am your mother. And I don't have the slightest idea what I'm doing. You are my first baby, my only son. I was just getting used to being pregnant, and now here you are! And you are so very, very real.

I've been preparing for your arrival for months. I've read the books. Well, some of them. A few pages. I've listened to my friends, who give me endless advice.

They're all experienced, you know, because they have their own babies. But you're different. You're my baby. And they don't know a thing about you.

I do. I know all about the way you kick and wiggle. I've already memorized the way you smell, like a fresh-from-the-earth daffodil. I know about the way your lower lip quivers when you're about to cry. I know that your wispy hair is the most luxuriously soft thing that has ever touched my cheek.

Yet I admit that there's much I don't know. In the hospital I had to be instructed how to nurse you. Yesterday my mother showed me how to bathe you in the sink. I don't have a clue how to clear up diaper rash. I get queasy at the sight of blood. I don't sew. I'm not good at salt dough maps. My math skills are atrocious. And you might as well know right up front that wiggly teeth give me the heebie-jeebies.

However, I am very good at baking cookies. I know how to make indoor tents on rainy days. And I have my father's wonderful sense of humor, so I know how to laugh and how to make you laugh.

I'll sing you sweet songs in the night. I'll pray for you every day. I'll let you keep any animal you catch, as long as you feed it. I'll call all your imaginary friends by their first names. I'll put love notes in your lunch box, and I'll swim with you in the ocean, even when I'm old. Perhaps the best thing about being your mother is that I get to share these privileges with the most incredible man in the world—your father.

Any credentials I have to offer can't be earned over coffee with friends…they can't be taught by a book. To me they are tender intuitions, whispers from God, eternal insights only a mother can know when her baby is cradled in her arms as you are now in mine. This is where the Lord will teach me how to mother you by heart.

SWEET DREAMS

Trade winds dancing with the palm trees,
Turquoise waves rushing to kiss the shore,
A fat, yellow moon winking at me,
Sweet baby asleep in my arms—
There is nothing else in the entire
world that I desire.

For Rachel

Rachel Elizabeth,
Little lamb, gift of God,
you came into this world so
fast and furious!
One moment I was gasping for air.
The next I pried my eyes open
and greeted your lizardlike pose
upon my chest.
Imagine!
You were just born and already
you held your head up,
blinking your eyes in the brightness.
I lifted my heavier-than-lead arms
to touch you and

your still-wet, trembling hand
clasped my eager finger.
Then you curled up into a
ten-pound ball of wailing flesh.

Today, at eighteen months,
you still come at me hard and fast.
I close my eyes for one moment
and there you are——
on top of the table, out the front door.
I'm exhausted from monitoring
your independence.
Such strength. Such determination.

Then comes a night like tonight
when you fight sleep,

TRUE A MOTHER HAS
MANY CARES, BUT THEY
ARE SWEET CARES.

JULIETTE MONTAGUE COOK

holding up that stiff neck so
assuredly until at last, in
my arms, you yield,
a twenty-pound ball of
helpless flesh.

My snuggly little lamb,
I smile at the future
for I know the Good Shepherd,
I hear His voice.
He makes you to lie down
in flannel crib sheets.
He restores my soul.
Surely goodness and mercy will
follow us all the days of our lives.

This Lord's Day

This Lord's Day,
I arose at six
prayed
showered
nursed the baby
fixed breakfast
dressed
ironed my husband's shirt
bathed the baby
dressed the baby
found my husband's watch
curled my hair
changed the baby's diaper
answered the phone
put on some makeup
stuck a roast in the oven
packed the diaper bag
grabbed my Bible
dashed to the kitchen for
Linda's casserole dish,
ran to the car and
as I strapped my little angel
into his car seat,
he vomited all over
everything, including me
and my only ironed dress.

Oh yes, Lord,
I shall remember this
Sabbath Day.
However, I must confess,
I am completely stumped
on how to keep it holy.

You surprise me.
You amaze me.
You razzle, dazzle, frazzle me!
And the only sure cure to get me by
Is if I laugh
Until I cry.

YOU KNOW YOU'RE A MOM WHEN YOU SAY

AT LEAST ONCE A DAY, "I'M NOT CUT OUT FOR THIS JOB," BUT

KNOW THAT YOU WOULDN'T TRADE IT FOR ANYTHING.

LIANE KUPFERBERG CARTER

MR. BOW TIE

When Young Ross was a year old, I bought him a navy blue bow tie for Easter. The clasps didn't work, so I strung elastic through it, and he wore it as proud as could be with the elastic hidden under his button-down collar.

He loved that bow tie.

One afternoon that summer he found the tie in his dresser drawer and took it with him all over the house, carrying it between his teeth like a dog bone. When I put him down for his nap, I changed him into a dry T-shirt, took the soggy thing out of his mouth, and placed it on the dresser top. He snuggled right down.

About twenty minutes later I heard a strange noise out front. I left the pile of laundry on the kitchen table and opened the door.

There was my little nap boy, wide-awake, riding his tricycle and wearing only (and I do mean only) a navy blue bow tie on an elastic string around his neck.

Can someone please tell me what this means?

WHO IS NOT ATTRACTED BY BRIGHT AND
PLEASANT CHILDREN, TO PRATTLE, TO CREEP,
AND TO PLAY WITH THEM?

JOHN LOCKE

Moment by Moment

We went to a barbecue today at the Kimber Park Pool. It was a gorgeous, hot Sunday afternoon. Sally and I stood by the picnic tables with our arms around each other, our warm cheeks pressed close, smiling as we posed and waited for Al to figure out why the camera wouldn't snap our picture.

There was a sudden commotion at the pool, thirty feet from where we stood.

The lifeguard was pulling out a toddler. It was my Rachel!

I raced to the pool, incredulous that she could have moved so fast in such short time. She had been clutching my leg all afternoon. When did she let go? Why didn't I realize it?

The lifeguard handed her to me. Her little pink Sunday dress dripped pool water down my leg. I held her close as she

coughed and coughed and then wailed with all the force of her twenty-month-old lungs. Everyone gathered around. She cried and cried. I sat down in a lounge chair, and she clung to me and whimpered. I wrapped her in a towel, and she fell asleep. When she woke up, she was all smiles and wanted me to push her on the swing.

It's now past two in the morning, and I can't sleep. Why didn't anyone tell me about this feeling? How many more times will this scene play itself over in my mind? When does it go away?

Forget everything anyone ever told me about how to be a good mother! I am at the mercy of a living, breathing God. He is the giver and sustainer of life.

Today He gave.

HER EYES ARE HOMES

OF SILENT PRAYER.

ALFRED LORD TENNYSON

MY FIVE-YEAR-OLD WARRIOR

I watch my five-year-old lower himself into the steaming tub where Mr. Bubble ministers to the wounds my son has suffered in battle today.

His arms bear scratches from the apple tree he scaled, and both knees are streaked with bloody reminders of his encounter with the sidewalk while charging on his trusty Huffy.

Gently I towel down his bruised thighs, which are dotted with bites from relentless mosquitoes.

With vigor I rough up his sun-bleached hair and shoo him into his room, where he dresses himself for bed.

A story, a prayer, a hug, and a kiss.

My brave warrior closes his eyes, and I stand back, marveling that this long, sturdy body, lying lumpy beneath the covers, once fit in my arms and nursed at my breast.

Many summer nights, just like this one, I rocked him. For hours I rocked and I sang and I prayed. Oh, how I prayed!

I close his door softly. My soldier needs his sleep.

Tomorrow great battles will be fought…in the sandbox, on his skateboard, with the neighborhood kids. He will return to me, bloodied and bruised, and there will be so little I can do. I have no power over scraped knees and stubbed toes.

But the real battle—the one not against flesh and blood but against principalities and powers of the air—has already begun in his young life. And in that battle, I am the warrior.

I pray.

Oh, how I pray!

That God will have the ultimate victory.

Today dawned like any other
And then "it" happened—
Completely unexpectedly.
I saw in you, through you, with you
A glimmer of heaven.

Autumn Dance

She stood a short distance from her guardian at the park this afternoon, her distinctive features giving away the fact that although her body blossomed into young adulthood her mind would always remain a child's. My children ran and jumped and sifted sand through perfect, coordinated fingers. Caught up in fighting over a shovel, they didn't notice when the wind changed. But she did. A wild autumn wind spinning the leaves into amber flurries. I called to my boisterous son and jostled my daughter. Time to go. Mom still has lots to do today. My rosy-cheeked boy stood still watching with wide-eyed fascination the gyrating dance of the Down syndrome girl as she scooped

up leaves and showered herself with a twirling rain of autumn jubilation. With each twist and hop she sang deep, earthy grunts—a canticle of praise meant only for the One whose breath causes the leaves to tremble from the trees. Hurry up. Let's go. Seat belts on? I start the car. In the rearview mirror I study her one more time through misty eyes. And then the tears come. Not tears of pity for her. The tears are for me. For I am too busy to dance in the autumn leaves and far too sophisticated to publicly shout praises to my Creator. I am whole and intelligent and normal, and so I weep because I will never know the severe mercy that frees such a child and bids her come dance in the autumn leaves.

PURE IN HEART

At church today I watched a daddy lift his son
to the wooden offering box.
The toddler leaned over and deposited
a fistful of change.
Straight blond hair in a bowl cut,
clear blue eyes; the toddler reminded me
of Young Ross at that age.
The boy turned to his daddy and asked,
"Is all this money for God?"
"Yes, it is," the father said.
The dad headed for the sanctuary.
The rascal in his arms wiggled and squealed,
"No, Daddy! Don't go yet! Wait there."
He pointed back at the offering box.
"I want to wait so I can see God when He comes
to get His money."

WE FIND DELIGHT IN THE BEAUTY AND

HAPPINESS OF CHILDREN THAT MAKES

THE HEART TOO BIG FOR THE BODY.

RALPH WALDO EMERSON

SURELY GOD LAUGHS

Yesterday Young Ross drew a special picture for Papa and Nana and found an envelope in the desk drawer. I caught him heading out the door with the bulky envelope clasped in his three-year-old fist.

I asked where he was going, and he said, "I go mailbox."

I told him he needed an address. The letter wouldn't get to Papa and Nana without an address. I told him to wait and I'd find the address for him right after lunch.

He handed me the envelope and scampered down the hall toward the bedrooms. I returned to the kitchen wondering why he had so willingly turned over the letter. I decided it must

be because of my clear explanation. That's all a kid needs. A little understanding, a little explanation about how letters must have addresses before they can be mailed…*crash!*

I ran to my bedroom and found him sprawled on the floor by the closet. Several dresses were draped over him. He had used an upside-down trash can to reach my clothes.

"What in the world are you doing?"

Unharmed, he held up a dress in each fist and announced, "Dis Papa's

Thank you, my little ones,
For bringing with you
Tender hearts and innocent eyes.
I love the way you sprinkle
your contagious giggles
All over my life.

dress. Dis Nana's dress. I go mailbox!"

I tumbled to the floor laughing and wrapped my arms around my silly little boy. He didn't understand my uncontrolled mirth or the tears cascading down my cheeks. But he embraced me wildly and kissed me, and together we laughed and laughed.

Later that evening I entered my invisible prayer closet. Suddenly, I saw myself as a spiritual toddler; full of determination, pulling down my own answers to prayers. How ridiculous I must look to God! What a bumbler!

Then I thought of my son and how my love for him sparkled that afternoon when he had tumbled into my laughing arms. It seemed quite possible that my heavenly Father is not disgusted or diappointed with me, after all. Maybe, as a loving parent, He watches me grow and delights in me simply because I am His child.

And maybe, sometimes, I make Him laugh.

*T*ODDLERS IN EDEN

This morning I listened from the upstairs nursery window to my four-year-old son and his little friend Asenath. After playing in the sandbox, they were now nestled together in the hammock, discussing what to play next.

Young Ross said he wanted to play Adam and Eve.

Asenath said no.

My son persisted, promising her it would be fun. He would be Adam, and she could be Eve.

No, Asenath didn't want to be Eve.

Young Ross asked then, who did she want to be?

Flipping back her golden curls, she said, "I want to be God."

My son-of-a-Gunn said, "Hey! That's just what the snake said! You can be the snake!"

I LOVE THESE LITTLE PEOPLE; AND IT IS NOT
A SLIGHT THING, WHEN THEY, WHO ARE
SO FRESH FROM GOD, LOVE US.

CHARLES DICKENS

DINNER OUTSIDE

One summer day we ate dinner outside on the back patio so we could enjoy the cool of the evening. I lifted Rachel out of her high chair so she and Young Ross could run barefoot in the grass. Ross and I sat and watched our kindergartner son being shadowed by his faithful sidekick, Rachel-the-Wonder-Two-Year-Old. She followed him underneath the overturned plastic wading pool. A moment later, the green, bottom-up pool began to scoot around the yard, propelled by four arms and four legs. Rachel's giggly voice called out, "It's cwazy twertle!"

We laughed. The pool stopped moving. We could hear the kids talking under their green dome, and we went back to our own conversation. A few minutes later Young Ross and Rachel popped up and rushed over to the table.

Young Ross said, "Go ahead, Rachel, tell them."

We waited.

Rachel laced her pudgy little fingers together and squeezed her eyes shut tight. "Dwr Desus."

"That's wonderful! Your big brother taught you how to pray, didn't he?" She opened her bright baby blues and nodded.

Cool, calm brother said, "Yeah, but she doesn't say all the words right, so I just went ahead and asked Jesus into her heart for her."

CHILDREN ARE GOD'S APOSTLES,

DAY BY DAY, SENT FORTH TO PREACH

OF LOVE, HOPE, AND PEACE.

JAMES RUSSELL LOWELL

Young heart, so brave,
So tender and true.
You came to me fresh from heaven
That I might learn of the
Father from you.

SURRENDER

Today as we left the baseball field after Young Ross's Little League practice, he and Rachel ran to the playground. I watched Ross steady Rachel's three-year-old legs as she climbed up the steps on the slide. He told her to wait while he ran around to the front. Then he opened his arms to catch her. I was impressed. Such a courteous young man. So considerate. So thoughtful. For a brief moment, I thought of how easy this motherhood thing was and patted myself on the back for raising two such delightful children.

Then a round girl with dark braids entered the sandy play area and headed for the slide. "Hey, I know you," my charming young man said. "Your mother works in the cafeteria at school."

The girl nodded shyly.

"Your mother is fat and ugly!" he said.

I froze. How could my own flesh and blood say such a thing!

I waited for my son to apologize to her. But he didn't. I scooped up Rachel and told Ross we were going to the car. He could join us after he apologized. I'd show him that he couldn't get away with this "sin" of rudeness. Sin separates us from God, and now his sin would separate him from me!

I marched off. Young Ross ran after me screaming, "Mommy, don't leave me!"

A man in his driveway rolled out from under his car, wrench in hand. He looked at me as if I were a child-beater. I calmly unlocked the car doors and settled Rachel in the front seat. Young

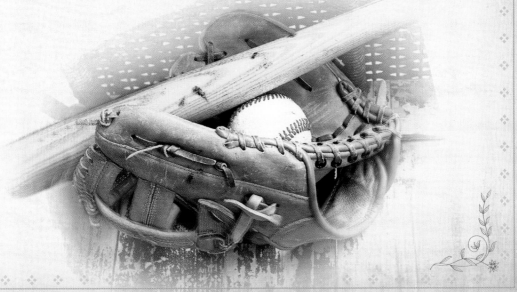

Ross had caught up and was wailing, "Mommy, what did I do?"

The mechanic's wife had now joined him in the driveway. Two other neighbors appeared across the street. I motioned for Young Ross to climb into the backseat.

The tears streamed down my son's face, yet I believed it was important that I bring this situation under control.

Calmly, I explained that it was rude to say the girl's mother was fat and ugly. "But she is!" Young Ross replied innocently. I told him that God made that little girl's mommy and that when Ross made fun of her, he was making fun of something God made.

His expression went from painful wincing to terrified sobriety. I was pleased with myself for clearing things up so easily and, I might add, spiritually. His humility was instant. Now we could leave.

Before I could close the door, Young Ross said, "Mommy, we need to pray." I told him we would when we got home.

No, he insisted. We must pray right here, right now, and he proceeded to climb out of the car and kneel on the muddy curb.

I was acutely aware of the half dozen people who were now watching. Rachel stood on the front seat, her big, round eyes peering over the headrest. Young Ross waited for me to join him on the muddy curb. Hands folded, honest eyes staring up at me, he expected me to kneel beside him.

Suddenly I understood what this was all about. This wasn't about my son and his sin of rudeness. This was about me and my need to always be right, to be in control. It was about my pride. My stubbornness. My sin.

I surrendered then. I had to. Down I went in front of God and the whole world. The mud felt cold on my knees.

I listened as my only son climbed up into the lap of our heavenly Father and told Him that he was sorry and promised to never again make fun of anything God made. Then, without questioning the Lord's instant forgiveness, Young Ross opened his eyes and hopped into the car.

I stayed frozen on that curb for another few eternal seconds, whispering my prayer. When I rose and found my way to the driver's side of the car, I was trembling inside and out.

Our curious audience continued to stare. I'm sure we were quite a spectacle. But I didn't care. Let them stare. Let my jeans get muddied knees. But, oh, Father, never let me become too proud to surrender as a child before You.

"Let the little children come to me, and do not hinder them, for the kingdom of God belongs to such as these."

MARK 10:14

ℒOVE LETTERS

One Sunday during the church service, Rachel sat next to me busily drawing on the back of an attendance card. She tugged on my sleeve and whispered could she please have a piece of very nice paper. I found in the back of my Bible a blank side of a hot pink bulletin insert. She was delighted.

I turned my attention back to the sermon and didn't look at her for a few minutes.

When I did, she was sitting completely still, with the paper and pencil balanced perfectly on her lap, her hands at her side. She was staring straight ahead, as if purposely not looking at the paper.

I was about to ask if she was okay, but then I noticed what she had written in her eight-year-old penmanship. The note read, "Do yu LOVE me? Yes/No." I'd seen these questions of

hers before. She wanted the answer circled, *Yes* or *No*.

I smiled and reached for the pencil to draw a big happy circle around the *Yes*. But she unfroze and snatched the pencil away from me. "I didn't write it to you," she whispered. I glanced at the person on the other side of her. I didn't know the woman. I doubted Rachel did.

"Who *did* you write it to?"

"God."

She placed the pencil back on the paper and waited without moving a muscle.

REAL TREASURE

We went to open house tonight at the elementary school. When Rachel's teacher met us, her eyebrows seemed to elevate slightly. She spoke kindly of our first-grader but said she had some concerns. She then invited us to look at the artwork; we would see what she meant.

Dozens of brown paper treasure chests were tacked to the bulletin board. Each had a barreled top attached with a brad. On the front was printed "A Real Treasure Would Be…." We walked over and began opening the lids to find Rachel's treasure and see why it so concerned the teacher.

As we peeked into each chest, we saw TVs and Nintendos, a few genies, heaps of gold coins, and a unicorn. Rachel's chest was in the very bottom corner. We had to stoop to open it. Inside, our daughter had drawn Christ, hanging on a cross with red drops of blood shaped like hearts dripping from his hands. She had completed the sentence, "A Real Treasure Would Be…Jesus."

"Do you see my concern?" the teacher asked, her arms folded across her chest.

"Yes," my husband replied. "I see what you mean. The J is backwards, isn't it?"

*I*NNOCENT PETITIONS

When we lived in Reno, Rachel had a best friend named Kristin. We moved to Portland only a few days before Rachel's first day of second grade. Each night we talked about her new school and prayed together before she went to bed. The night before school started, Rachel prayed that Jesus would give her a new best friend at this school and that her name would be Kristin. I felt compelled to alter her prayer but decided to let it go. How could I tell my child that she shouldn't be so specific with God?

The next morning Rachel stood quietly in front of the mirror while I combed her hair. She suddenly announced that Jesus was going to give her a new best friend. Her name would be Kristin, and she would have brown hair, just like the Kristin in Reno.

I quickly ran through all my mental notes on prayer. What would be the best way to explain to this child that prayer is not telling God what we have in mind for Him to do, but rather seeking His mind? I tried a few flimsy

FOR MOTHER'S SAKE THE CHILD WAS DEAR, AND DEARER WAS THE MOTHER FOR THE CHILD.

SAMUEL TAYLOR COLERIDGE

sentences. All fell flat. Rachel seemed undaunted. I drove her to school still unable to find a way to protect her from her own prayer. I was afraid that she would experience a real spiritual crisis when she arrived at school and found no brunette Kristin in her class. What would that do to her innocent faith?

We entered the classroom, and Rachel found her name on her new desk. As she lifted the top and began to examine the contents, I saw out of the corner of my eye the name of the student who would occupy the desk next to Rachel. There, printed in bold black letters was the name Kristin.

I could barely speak. "Rachel," I finally managed in a whisper. "Look! There is a Kristin in your class. And she's going to sit right next to you!"

"I know, Mom. She's the one I prayed for."

At that moment the bell rang. Feeling a bit stunned I walked to the back

of the classroom as the students began to come in. Rachel sat up straight, folded her hands on her desk, and grinned confidently.

I glued my eyes to that door. Four boys entered. Then a girl with blond hair who took a seat in the first row. Two more boys and, then, there she was! She sauntered shyly to the desk labeled "Kristin," caught Rachel's welcoming grin, and returned the same.

I probably don't need to mention that she had brown hair down to her waist. Or that everything I really need to know about prayer I learned when Rachel started second grade.

Faith brings us on highways that make our reasoning dizzy.
CORRIE TEN BOOM

IF YOU WANT A HAPPY FAMILY,

IF YOU WANT A HOLY FAMILY,

GIVE YOUR HEARTS TO LOVE.

MOTHER TERESA

THE FATHER'S PLEASURE

Today the wind invited the children and me outside to chase it. So we did. The trees, like dancing gypsies with jewels in their hair, laughed above us as we frolicked down the street. The pockets of my jacket began to fill with autumn treasures, placed there by two sets of small hands.

Returning to the warm house, red faced and breathless, the children dumped their goodies onto the kitchen table, giddy with the joy of discovery. Along with several twigs and many rocks, Young Ross had bagged a snail's shell—minus one snail. Rachel laid out each of her big, amber-colored leaves, then chose the largest one to use as a fan. I watched them as they arranged and rearranged each acorn, rock, leaf, and twig, preparing their own centerpiece for the table. The children spoke in hushed tones, lost in wonder, mesmerized by a handful of God's trinkets.

It reminded me of when I was young. I would regularly bring home treasures to my mother and scatter them across the kitchen counter. One afternoon her hand passed over the tiny white pebbles and squashed red geraniums extracted from my pockets to stop at a tattered gray feather. I had almost left the spiny thing in the gutter since it appeared broken and useless.

Mom ran her fingers up the feather's tattered sides and turned it toward the kitchen window. Soft hues of sunshine lit the feather, changing it from dull gray to bright silvery-blue as she twirled it between her fingers, a marvelous wonder to my young eyes. An "ordinary" miracle.

With fumbling words I entered my children's moment of wonder and told them how much God dearly treasured them. I wanted them to feel, in that moment, the pleasure of the Father, to understand how He delights in collecting the ordinary of this world and bringing it into the warmth of His kingdom. How His touch can turn the tattered into the dazzling.

Most of all, I wanted my children to know that their young hearts are not trinkets to be played with but are rare, priceless jewels in the hands of the King.

They looked at me with innocent eyes, unaffected by my intense lecture. Had I once looked at my own mother the same way?

Maybe such eternal truths can't really be taught, I decided. They can only be collected, examined, arranged, rearranged—and finally treasured. And this takes a lifetime of days filled with ordinary miracles.

EVERY CHILD BORN INTO THE WORLD IS A
NEW THOUGHT OF GOD, AN EVER-FRESH
AND RADIANT POSSIBILITY.

KATE DOUGLAS WIGGIN

THE WISH BENEATH MY PILLOW

This morning I was cleaning closets and discovered a small, unmarked box on my son's top shelf. I placed it on the edge of the bed. It toppled over, its contents spilling onto the floor. The first thing I saw was a tiny blue tennis shoe. "His first pair of running Nikes," my brother had written on the gift card. I picked up the unbelievably small shoe and held it in the palm of my hand. I couldn't help but compare. Reaching inside the closet I extracted one smelly high-top tennis shoe. I held the infant shoe next to the toddler tennie. The contrast was mind-boggling.

Tonight I looked at my son's feet as he came to dinner. I peeked at them under the table twice. I watched him walk up the stairs. When I tucked him in bed, I grabbed his right foot and gave it a playful wrangle. It no longer fit in the palm

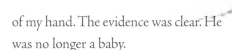

of my hand. The evidence was clear. He was no longer a baby.

After my son was asleep, I slipped into my bedroom and retrieved the baby shoe, which I'd hidden among my socks that afternoon. Nobody saw me press the silly little thing to my cheek. All I could think about was how I longed for another pair of feet around this house. A pair of feet tiny enough to fit into these infant shoes….

I thought of how my mother's generation delighted in bronzing our baby shoes and mounting them on the mantle. In that prominent place the shoe served as a visual reminder that children are tiny for such a short breath of time. Perhaps, at times, they also represented the wish for another tiny pair of feet in that home….

I didn't want to put my little blue shoe on display. At least not yet. Tonight it was still my secret discovery—a poignant reminder for my heart alone.

With the tiny shoe still pressed against my cheek, I closed my eyes and made a wish. Then I tucked my secret wish under my pillow and waited for it to come true.

There is a time for everything,
and a season for every
activity under heaven:
a time to be born and a time to die,
a time to plant and a time to uproot,
a time to embrace
and a time to refrain.

ECCLESIASTES 3:1–2, 5B

$\mathcal{H}$OLDING BACK TIME

The kids and I went up to the lake today, eager to escape the heat. We settled in the sand at Kings Beach, and off Rachel and Young Ross ran to play in the water.

I heard some girls giggling and scanned the shoreline until I saw three bikini-clad junior high girls splashing water at a boy and running away before he could splash them back. Of course they returned for more splashes and more carefree giggling.

Ah, youth!

Under the August sun I wiggled my toes into the sand and thought back on my wonder years when my sister and I spent our summers innocently flirting with the boys at the beach. We were just like those girls, all arms and legs, chasing boys. Teasing them. Diligently planning our attacks until we got one of them to respond.

I smiled at those adorably skinny girls, feeling a sense of sisterhood. Of camaraderie. I marveled at the timeless elixir of sand, sun, and shore. Of how it is mixed vigorously by the summer wind and poured out on innocents, whisking them from childhood to adulthood. I watched as the skipping, giggling girls honed in on their unsuspecting victim and…

Suddenly I sprang from my chair.

Those girls weren't flirting with boys! They were chasing my boy, my baby! Why those…those…hussies! How dare they? You little flirts! Get away from him! Do you hear me? Shoo! Go away!

Certainly my son would not respond to such immature antics.

But he was.

He was splashing them back, smiling and looking manly with his chest all puffed out and his hands on his hips. The summer wind was shamelessly at work, right before my eyes, enticing my boy into puberty. He shouldn't respond yet, should he? He's only eleven.

Eleven?

Eleven!

When did he turn eleven?

I shielded my eyes from the sun with my arm and continued to stare. I refused to blink. I didn't dare. I knew if I closed my eyes for even one second, my baby boy would suddenly be transformed into a man.

ONLY BOYS FROM DAY TO DAY

CAN DRAIN AND FILL THE CUP OF PLAY;

THAT AGE MUST MOURN FOR WHAT IS LOST

THROUGHOUT THE COMING YEARS.

BUT BOYS CANNOT APPRECIATE

THEIR PRICELESS JOY UNTIL TOO LATE,

AND THOSE WHO OWN THE CHARMS I HAD

WILL SOON BE CHANGED TO MEN;

AND THEN, THEY TOO WILL SIT, AS I,

AND BACKWARD TURN TO LOOK AND SIGH

AND SHARE MY LONGING, VAIN,

TO BE A CAREFREE BOY AGAIN.

EDGAR GUEST

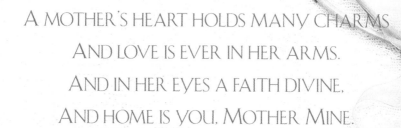

A MOTHER'S HEART HOLDS MANY CHARMS
AND LOVE IS EVER IN HER ARMS.
AND IN HER EYES A FAITH DIVINE,
AND HOME IS YOU, MOTHER MINE.

AUTHOR UNKNOWN

LIKE MOTHER, LIKE DAUGHTER

Rachel came home from school today with Kristin's phone number—memorized! This is a first. I watch her march to the portable phone and say the number aloud as she dials.

"Hello. This is Rachel Gunn. May I please speak to Kristin?"

She balances the phone on her shoulder, just the way I do, and begins to walk around the house. I don't look like that, do I?

"Hi, Kristin. It's Rachel." She opens the cupboard and checks for snacks, still balancing the phone.

"Nothing. What are you doing?"

She heads for the front porch with a handful of pretzels.

I call out after her, "Would you like something to drink?"

She half turns and, with a sweet facial expression and a finger touched to her lips, silently motions for me not to interrupt her. Is that what I do?

I casually follow her to the porch and nestle on the wicker love seat. I begin flipping through a magazine. Rachel's eyes meet mine, and she gives me a "don't you have anything better to do than follow me around all day?" look.

She speaks. Not to me, but to that invisible person on the phone. "I remembered your number."

She checks the hanging petunias with her free hand to see if they need water. There she is, balancing the phone on her shoulder, clutching pretzels with her right hand, and fingering the soil with her left. Just like her mother.

"Well, that's all. I guess I'll see you tomorrow at school."

She wipes her muddy finger on a leaf, still balancing the phone. Then clutching her wad of pretzels, she pulls a wicker chair toward her with her foot—just like I do.

"Okay. Bye."

I watch as Rachel pulls the phone away from her ear with her free hand, then catches a pretzel between her teeth and presses the off button with her nose. Just like....

"Do you know what?" I tell her as she joins me on the love seat and tries to fit her preadolescent body onto my lap. "Do you know that I think you're absolutely amazing?"

She smiles, kisses me on the tip of my nose, and says, "I know. That's 'cause I'm just like you."

Rachel,
I've come to a decision.
Don't try to change my mind.
Your birthday shall be canceled.
You shall be forever
Nine!

DEEP, CLEANSING BREATHS

Donna and I went shopping with our daughters today. Her Natalie is sixteen; my Rachel is eight. The excursion went something like this:

Natalie pulls a few bathing suits off the rack. Donna begins taking several deep, cleansing breaths, which strangely resemble the breathing techniques we were taught in our childbirth classes years ago. We head for the dressing room. Rachel reaches for a few more swimsuits for Natalie to try on, and the two young ladies disappear behind the thick, blue curtain.

A few moments later, Rachel's round face appears. She asks if we want to see. Of course we do. Back goes the curtain, and there stands Natalie in a bathing suit that slides over her every curve. Donna holds her breath until Natalie says she doesn't like it. I hear Donna letting out a "hee, hee, hee, whew."

Natalie returns to the dressing room. I watch the clock. It's about three minutes between changes. Rachel pulls back the curtain and displays suit number two on her life-sized Barbie model. This one is a two-piece. Donna's breathing has turned noticeably more rapid.

Two minutes now between changes. We see suit number three, a rather low-cut black number. Donna begins sucking air in through clenched teeth. She seems a tad irritable, as if this transition is harder on her than it is on Natalie.

Here comes suit number four. Donna's face is red. She's clutching the sides of the chair and doesn't appear to be breathing at all. The curtain closes, and a stream of controlled breath passes through Donna's cracked lips. I consider going for ice chips, but it won't be long now, and I don't want to miss the grand conclusion. I coach Donna, telling her to hang in there. Just one more.

Rachel whips back the curtain, and Natalie turns around in number five, a lovely yet modest one-piece.

Donna's whole body pushes up from the chair, and with all her strength she announces, "That's the one!" Everyone is pleased. We all congratulate each other. I pass around a roll of LifeSavers.

Thus I came to know and understand the real reason they teach us Lamaze. It has nothing to do with the infant in the delivery room. It's all about the teenage daughter in the dressing room.

WHAT A MOTHER SAYS

Oh, let me hold her!
Hush, my little angel.
Aren't you sleepy yet?
It's okay. Don't cry.
Come to Mommy.
Take that out of your mouth. Yucky!
Tell mommy if you need to go
    potty, okay?
Don't get into your brother's things.
Get back in bed.
I just brought you a drink of water.
Pick up your toys.
Go wash your hands.

Can you remember to bring it
    home tomorrow?
Did you practice?
I'm sure she still wants to be
    your friend.
Try looking under your bed.
Stop teasing your brother.
Where was it when you last saw it?
Go clean your room.
Come set the table.
Don't bite your nails.
Did you do your homework?
Tell her you'll call her back.

HOW MANY DO HIS PARENTS
YOU'RE NOT OLD   HAVE ON THE GUEST LIST?
ENOUGH YET.
THERE'S A BOY ON THE
PHONE FOR YOU.

WHEN DO WE GET TO MEET HIM?

Who else is going?
You may not wear that to school.
Did you tell me it was this Saturday?
There's a boy on the phone for you.
No, I need the car this afternoon.
Are you coming home this weekend?
    Next weekend?
When do we get to meet him?
Yes. I understand why you changed
    your major.
No. What you're feeling is normal.
The photographer is here.

Don't sit on your veil.
Oh, let me hold you one more time.
Call us when you get there.
Good-bye, my baby girl.

WE LOVE YOU, TOO,
SWEETHEART.

WHAT A MOTHER THINKS

I love you so much.
There is no way I can possibly put into
words how proud I am of you.
You're absolutely beautiful.
Sometimes when our eyes meet,
it's like gazing into a reflecting pool.
I see in you glimmers of my past.
Do you see in me hints of your future?
You are everything I ever prayed for.
I love you more than you will ever know,
more than you will ever ask.
There's nothing I wouldn't give for you,
nothing I wouldn't do for you.
You are my daughter,
and I will always love you with a love so
immense, so eternal…
I could never find a way to squeeze it
into words.

What a Daughter Thinks

My mother doesn't understand me.
She never has,
and she never will.

MOTHER MEANS SELFLESS DEVOTION,

LIMITLESS SACRIFICE,

AND LOVE THAT PASSES UNDERSTANDING.

AUTHOR UNKNOWN